Bosom
Buddies

Also by Deborah McKinlay

Love Lies
Sex Secrets

Bosom Buddies

BEYOND GIRLS' TALK

What Women Do
(and Men Don't)

Deborah McKinlay

HarperCollins*Publishers*

Illustrations by Josephine Sumner

HarperCollins*Publishers*
77–85 Fulham Palace Road,
Hammersmith, London W6 8JB

Published by HarperCollins*Publishers* 1996
1 3 5 7 9 8 6 4 2

A catalogue record for this book is
available from the British Library

ISBN 0 00 255776 2

Set in Berkeley Book

Printed and bound in Great Britain by
Caledonian International Book Manufacturing Ltd, Glasgow

This book is dedicated to

Sandra Coppen
Kirsten Cortizo
Claire Davis
Jane De Groen
Abigail Eaton
Jane Lawson
Claire Lewis
Nadja Ray
Rebecca Reed
and
Diana Sieff

As fine a set of bosoms as you could ever hope to come across

CONTENTS

When a Woman calls another Woman
She doesn't need a reason

1

Mange Too

....

'Could you tell me about the puddings, please?'
'We have a wonderful chocolate mousse, a selection of sorbets, a fruit tart, a creme caramel, and an excellent ginger ice cream made by our own kitchen'
'Uh-huh ... which one's the biggest?'

....

Women meet for lunch because things are going well for one of them. Or because things are not going so well for one of them. Or because it's Wednesday.

WOMEN'S THINGS-GOING-WELL DEFINITION

New man
New marriage (any step towards this state)
New money (any source)
New body
New baby (if it occurs with the right combination of the above)
Fabulous new glamorous type of career with lots of lunching
    opportunities (bound to lead to some of the above)

WOMEN'S THINGS-NOT-GOING-SO-WELL DEFINITION

Distinct lack of any of the above

Outward signs of the first are:

New hairdo
New outfit

Outward signs of the second are:

Distinct lack of any of the above

Women never want to sit about in public places on their own. If the public place in question is a public bar, this is partly due to the possibility of unwelcome advances from unattractive men. (Most women will welcome a wee bit more, advance-wise, from attractive men. Most men are not in the dark about this.) But, actually, the real reason a woman is wary of arriving at a rendezvous too much in advance is that she doesn't want it to look like she's been stood up.

A woman who has arrived on time (i.e. five minutes late) for lunch is a wee bit disappointed when the grinny restaurant door person shows her to an empty table. The woman kills a bit of time trying to get her handbag to hang on the back of her chair and then gives up and puts it under the seat. She looks at the door. No one she knows is coming through it. She drags her handbag out again and does some twiddling with it. Eventually, she removes a tissue and puts it in her pocket. She looks at the door. No one she knows is coming through it. When she orders a large bottle of mineral water the smile she gives the waiter has a slight nervy edge.

The woman worries a bit, while she is sipping her mineral water, re: place/date/time.

Then she begins to get irritated.

These reactions alternate with gathering intensity until, at last, she looks at the door and sees someone she knows coming through it.

A woman who has arrived late (i.e. more than fifteen minutes) for lunch approaches the table, all wreathed in apologetic smiles. She's full of breathy excuses while she's fiddling with her hand-bag.

By the time she takes a sip of her mineral water her friend has forgiven her completely.

When a woman is lunching with just one other woman whom she knows well, ordering is fairly straightforward.

They both scan the specials in a half-hearted sort of way and then one of them says: 'I've been rushing around all morning. I haven't had a chance to eat *anything*.'

The other woman looks relieved and says: 'Me too.'

This is a tacit agreement to order the most piggy thing on the menu. In girls' restaurants this is something with the word 'fried' written next to it in a foreign language.

When women are lunching in a group, or a not so intimate twosome, things can be a bit more tricky. Because ... a woman doesn't want to be the *only* one to order something piggy.

A woman who is carrying a kilo or fifteen more than any of the women she's lunching with *never* orders something piggy.

Genuine big and bad, in-your-face, female, food-flaunting attitude only comes with mega self-discovery. A fair few of the going-well ingredients are usually in evidence as well.

Sometimes one of the women has gained a bit of bottom since she lunched with her chums on the third Wednesday of the month before last. Often, things are not going so well for this woman.

> Woman-land is full of magic kilos. No one can see them except not-going-well women. No matter how publicly the not-going-well women parade their magic kilos ('Look, look, these trousers were *loose*, last year') everyone just says, 'You do *not* look fat.'
>
> Magic kilos melt miraculously away once a woman's life regains a little zest (see Women's going-well definition).

The woman with the thigh anxiety sighs and orders something salad sounding. She's mildly irritated if a pin-skinny girl (swish new hair cut and immaculate monochrome outfit) asks for extra *frites*.

Lunching women drink wine. Even those who imbibe pretty seriously are much more likely to pour a couple of litres of chablis or champagne down their throats than order a neat scotch in front of the other girls.

Not-going-well women *never* order a neat scotch in front of the other girls.

Women talk constantly while they are eating their curly lettuce leaves. At least one of them is talking at any time. They laugh a lot but they don't tell jokes, they tell stories.

> Men think that women talk about trivia. This is not strictly true. Women simply include all the trivial aspects of whatever they're talking about. They like *Details*.

The Talking Round is fairly obstacle free.

Women rarely argue openly, especially in a group. If one of the women says something which gets up the nose of one of the other women, the offendee is likely to say nothing. Later she calls an ally and they have a good forty-five minute session about it.

Pudding is negotiated along pretty much the same lines as the initial order. Mostly women go for the safe option, i.e. eschewing the *tarte tatin* and having a cappuccino instead.

CAPPUCCINO DRINKING: THE RULES

The women say No, no they couldn't possibly manage a pudding. They'll just have a cappuccino (extra chocolate).

The cappuccino is served in big white cups with too-small handles and the women often have to wipe the drippy bits off with their napkins.

They wolf them down.

They coyly lick the last vestiges of the frothy stuff off their teaspoons.

Until (at last) someone says, 'Have you got time for another cappuccino?'

There is a general sigh of relief, everyone looks at their watches.

There is a little chorus of 'Oh, yes. OK.'

Someone signals the waiter.

The waiter doesn't need to come to the table to find out what the women want.

Girls' restaurant waiters (i.e. part-time models) know the routine.

LEAVING THE RESTAURANT

No one wants to leave first.

No one wants to leave alone.

This is because a woman suspects that the other women will talk about her. They probably will.

In a worst case lunch-leaving scenario one woman has to head back to work while the others Go Shopping.

2

Till You Drop

'They haven't got it in my size'
'Get it anyway, it's such *a bargain*'

Women like to shop.
Women like to shop in pairs.

What a woman wants a shopping companion for:

- To find something that would suit her, or go with something she's already got that she might have missed
- To tell her that something that she hasn't missed, suits her and will go with something she's already got
- To say 'Let's have a cappuccino'
- To assuage her guilt

Women tend to feel guilty about their shopping because, secretly, they suspect that it is not very grown-up to buy sling-backs when the gas bill is due. The good shopping companion plays along with the idea that the purchaser *needs* a new pair of sling-backs. They discuss this at length over the cappuccino. The purchaser generally manages to convince the companion that she needs something too. They go back for it after the cappuccino.

One thing that a shopping companion does not do is to comment on

THE TRYING-ON FACE

Many women inherit a Trying-On Face from their mothers (this idea horrifies any right-thinking female).

A woman may have little trying-on gestures which go with the Trying-On Face. She does these in the cramped, curtained booth with the three-way mirrors. (These often afford a view of her thighs and bottom which leaves her sighing.) The companion squishes in the hallway holding the handbags.

People who have children find out about their Trying-On Face. It is the job of children to master a perfect imitation of their mother's Trying-On Face complete with gestures.

When both women have spent their gas bill and are having a last little wander about (casually leafing through the sale racks just in case there is something they've missed which would go with something that they've already got and that they *need*), one woman says: 'Poor Kate.'

And the other one says: 'Oh I know.'

Then they spend an hour and a half in animated discussion about how well things are not going for Kate.

Sometimes they have to have another cappuccino somewhere in order thoroughly to explore all the possibilities of this conversation.

When the women reach the point where the conversation has gone full circle several times like a Muzak recording; when the women give up on trying to get the part-time model to bring them a piece of carrot cake (they decided to share one with their second cappuccino); when neither of the women suggests *another* cappuccino, and the froth-licking possibilities have been completely exhausted ... they go home.

Once they are separated they start to feel a bit sick.
They regret the second cappuccino.
They regret some of the beans they spilled about Kate.
They have a teeny tiny second thought about the pink shirt.

They feel the onset of severe panic with regard to the gas bill.

When a woman has spent all her gas bill money on a pair of pale blue sling-backs and a pink silk shirt suitable for wearing to a pool party in southern California, she feels a bit upset when she notices these items lingering, unworn, in the back of her wardrobe in the mornings.

She feels even more upset when she sees the final gas bill reminder, lying unpaid on the hall table.
She channels all this upset into an irate tirade about the *ridiculous* cost of gas.
Sometimes she feels a bit better after she has treated some hapless gas-board employee to this tirade.

The other thing that makes women feel much better about particularly useless purchases in the clothing line is trying them on, i.e. Dressing Up.

DRESSING UP IN UNSUITABLE PURCHASES IN THE CLOTHING LINE

[NB This behaviour is not limited to the loony fringe]
Women under the age of twenty-one do it together.

Requirements

- A mirror (full length preferably, otherwise the Dresser Upper is forced to clamber onto the bed, or in worst case scenarios, the loo seat, for a better view)
- Liquid sustenance (wine is wonderful but tea will do)
- Stereo
- Extremely detailed fantasy image of a pool party in southern California.

A woman who is spending a wet Saturday night alone in a basement flat in Putney, dressing up in all the unworn items in her wardrobe (between dancing and accompanying Aretha on the harmony bits), is able to picture her own entrance to this party so vividly that she can convince herself she *needs* to buy some earrings to go with the pink silk shirt.

Men sometimes accuse women of living in a fantasy world.

3

Once Upon a Time

....

lavender bath oil
eye make-up remover
firming eye cream
toner
moisturising shower gel
hot-oil hair conditioner
mud masque
body lotion
peppermint foot spray
replenishing night cream
thigh-thinning massage treatment
cleanser (creamy)
cleanser (rinse off)
lip balm
depilatory cream
oatmeal exfoliating scrub (for the face)
seaweed exfoliating scrub (for the body)
styling spray
shampoo-in colour (lasts six washes)
nail polish remover

Once a woman has stocked up on a few essentials she has a bit less space for cough mixture in her bathroom cupboard than a man does

....

A woman knows what she would wear if she won an Oscar.

A woman knows what your flat would look like if she lived in it.

A woman knows exactly what she would do with the lottery money.

Women share this imaginary world with their friends. When a woman says something like: 'I'm not sure I'd actually *live* in the Winner's Luxury Dream Cottage, it might be smarter to rent it out for now ...' another woman can pick up the thread.

Women's fantasies are as detailed as their conversations. Women's ability to fantasise enables them to imagine that if they just lost a kilo or three, bought a new lipstick and found some earrings to go with that pink shirt ... they would look like Demi Moore.

Women are able to summon this type of fantasy image whilst queuing to pay for half a cabbage (with unwashed hair and a pair of brown leggings clinging to their unshaven calves). Fantasies keep women sane.

Women's fantasies are what fuel the Hope in a Jar Industry.

Some smart people have got *very rich* on account of the Hope in a Jar Industry.

These people understand that women know that there is no such thing as a Nano-Zanosphere. Women *don't care*.

When a woman shops for beauty products she generally goes it alone. A woman will discuss, at length, the benefits of the newest Nano-Zanosphere Complex with her nearest and dearest friends.

A woman knows which particular Nano-Zanosphere Complex is currently favoured by her nearest and dearest friends, but the actual expedition-to-purchase is often a solo venture.

A woman over the age of twenty-one has usually begun to carve out her own trail in the Nano-Zanosphere jungle.

'I've only been using it for three months but the *difference ...*'

Still, sometimes she needs a guide.

If a woman hesitates in the Nano-Zanosphere jungle a Sherpa soon appears.

Nano-Zanosphere Sherpas ...

- wear a uniform of smock and matching lipstick
- speak special Nano-Zanosphere lingo

An example of Nano-Zanosphere lingo: 'A breakthrough micro-sphere with an exclusive bio-crystal texture.'

When the woman hears a smattering of this lingo she feels confident of the Sherpa's superior knowledge. She proceeds to tell this creature everything about herself. They have a long discussion about dry patches and thread veins.

After a bit, the Sherpa brings out from her Survival Pack an array of little pots of potion. She carefully removes the lid from one of these pots and gently takes the woman's hand in hers. She smears a little of the potion on the back of the woman's hand. They both gaze at this hand in awed silence for a few moments.

It is not long after this that the woman gives the Sherpa her credit card.

Women don't spend their house insurance money on derivatives of cow's placenta and rub it on their faces just because they *believe* that this process will make them look beautiful. They do it because it makes them feel grown up.

Small female people consider rubbing cream on your face to be a ritual of adulthood. They get to do it at about the same time as small male people get to shave. Shaving cream is a bit cheaper.

Very few men have the remotest idea of just how much cheaper, very few women would want them to find out.

The woman leaves the Nano-Zanosphere jungle alone but confident. She is carrying a very small bag. This bag represents about a month's salary.

Women do not allow lack of cash to keep their Hope in a Jar fantasies down. If a gal really can't find the funds ('She cut up my card ... right in front of me') for a Nano-Zanosphere need, she can always turn to the honey pot for comfort, or the fruit bowl, or the cereal packet ('You just mix the oats with the yoghurt and slap it on').

Kitchen sink beauty tips are often shared with friends: 'What do I do with the cucumber?'

Many men would find it difficult to imagine what it is that women find enjoyable about lying around the sitting room with egg on their faces, but then *they've* never experienced the bonding effects of pouring beer on each other's hair.

After a bit of beautifying women are often full of beans. Even if the Demi Moore look-alike progress hasn't been quite as rapid as they'd hoped ('Well ... it *feels* amazing'), they don't want all their efforts to go to waste. They want to put on their glad rags and strut their stuff.

No one has been invited to a pool party in southern California, so they plan a bit of a night on the town instead.

The women pour themselves a glass of wine, put the stereo on full blast, accompany Aretha on all the harmony bits and try on all the unworn outfits in their wardrobes.

They settle on something entirely unsuitable for trying to find a cab in at 3 am on a windy high street.

4

The Feeling's Mutual

'So, what's he like?'
  'He's ... you know, he's a good guy'
  'He's nice?'
  'Yeah. I guess'
  'What does he do?'
  'He's an architect'
  'No, no. I know that. I mean, what are his interests?'
  'I dunno ... football'
  'What else?'
  'I dunno'
  'What does he look like?'
  'What does he look like? Whaddya mean, what does he look like?
He's got hair, he's got a nose ... he's a bloke ...'

A woman generally finds it easier to get the necessary
information from another woman.

A woman leaves her house on a Saturday night. Her hair is done
in a close approximation of a style she saw in a magazine feature
called 'Sleek and Chic.' Her lipstick is Sinful Cinnamon. Her
tights are new, so is at least one of the other garments that she is
wearing.

The woman has a teeny tiny doubt about her choice of shoes when her feet first hit the pavement, but she is buoyed up again once she meets the other girls and they all tell each other how fab they look.

The evening only really starts to go downhill when someone says: 'Oooh, no, let's not go *there* again.'

Later, when they have been to quite a few places ('Come on, you can't dance to *this*') and had quite a few drinks ('We'll just have one drink here and then we'll go') the woman goes to the loo.

She notices that there's a snag in her tights. The rest of her is looking a little less 'Sleek and Chic' too. Sinful isn't in it.

The woman takes her comb out of her handbag, sighs and says: 'I'm getting too old for this.'

The woman who has gone to the loo with her finishes re-touching her lipstick and says: 'Me too, we'll just have one more drink and then we'll go, shall we?'

Women spend a few years going out simply for an excuse to dress up. Then they decide that they have outgrown this phase. They keep buying outfits suitable for getting-dressed-up-and-going-out in for quite some time after this happens.

Women who've got to the stage in life where they no longer feel comfortable on the No. 9 night bus wearing over-the-knee boots, start to favour different sorts of evening get-togethers.

At 8 pm on any Thursday, of any week, of any month, of any year, a million women are sitting on other women's sofas, eating pasta off forks.

The women, whose sofa it isn't, have brought bottles of wine. These bottles are open. The women are wearing their work clothes. (In close friendships leggings may make an appearance.)

Sometimes a party has a point ... ('Thirty-three, so it's not like a major celebration') in which case medium-level dressing-up is required (nothing new, reasonably comfy shoes) and the women bring presents as well as wine.

But, mostly, they are just an excuse to get together and have a good old gas.

Pasta Party conversation isn't hampered by interruptions from part-time model waiters. Also, sofas are more accommodating to extra bits of bottom than twiddly, girls' restaurant chairs are. The women are very relaxed.

One of the women goes to the loo. She doesn't bother to fiddle with her hair. When she gets back she fancies a cup of coffee, so she just goes right to the kitchen and makes some for everyone.

Gal-pal Thursday nights in are lovely.

When the women, whose sofa it wasn't, are getting ready to go, and someone's mini-cab has arrived, they give each other a hug. They are very affectionate. They say: 'Call me on the weekend.'

That night, when they're cleaning their teeth and slapping on their Nano-Zanospheres, they think: 'Women friends are just the *best*.'

Women do all the things for their women friends that they wish men would do for them.

These are some of the things:

- Tell them that they look nice (after they've used the Nano-Zanosphere Complex)
- Tell them that they look nice (when they're wearing the pink shirt)
- Give them what they want for their birthdays
- Give them flowers, even if it isn't their birthday
- Call them on the weekend

One Thursday a woman arrives at a Pasta Party wearing a bit of a swish new monochrome outfit. She is grinning from ear to ear. The other women grin too.

'Still going well, then?' they ask.

'Oooh, yes, he's *wonderful*,' says the woman, 'and look, I've lost two kilos.'

New Man Syndrome can play havoc with women's gal-pal relationships ...
Things women suffering from New Man Syndrome have been known to do to another woman:

- Cut a telephone conversation short, in case He calls
- Cut a shopping expedition short, in case He calls
- Pull out of a Pasta Party, because He did call
- Forget to thank her for her birthday present, because He didn't call

But mostly the effects aren't terminal ...
Because there is a tacit agreement in woman-land that anything to do with a New Man is probably more important than 'just us girls stuff.'

All the women have a good gas about the New Man. They want *Details*. They give the grinny woman a right grilling. The Pasta Party sofa talk develops a saucy edge. When the woman with the New Man goes to the loo all the women say: 'I'm so glad things are going a bit better for Kate.' And they are.

Unless ...
Kate's New Man turns out to be a right rat-bag and Kate 'Just cannot see it.'
Or ...
Kate has New Man Syndrome attacks on a regular basis ('You'd think she'd *learn*').

There is another circumstance in which New Man Syndrome can have negative side effects for an onlooker.

Sometimes, with the exception of minor birthday celebrations, the Pasta Party set is pretty small. In fact, it's a Double Act.

When two women get really familiar with each other's sofas their friendship becomes very cosy indeed.

These two always call each other on the weekend.

They decide which movie they want to see.

They decide not to eat junk this weekend.

They decide not to spend any money this weekend.

They decide that popcorn is quite healthy really.

They decide that popping into Pellini's Pizza and Pasta for a cinema supper would be easier than searching for something edible at the Eight 'til Late.

They decide to have another cappuccino.

Over the cappuccino the women have a good old gas. Later, when they have slapped on their Nano-Zanospheres and set the alarm for Monday morning, they don't like to think about how the weekend might have gone without a chum to share and care with.

On Thursday night, one of these women shows up at the other woman's house wearing an ear-to-ear grin and a Sleek and Chic new hairdo.

And then there was one.

5

Male and Interesting

···

Soon after a woman begins a new romance, some very comfortable clothes get shoved to the back of her wardrobe.

···

'He's been really down lately'
'Uh huh'
'I think things are a bit tricky at the office. I'm quite worried about him'
'Right'
'Last night he was awake half the night. He said he had stomach pains but I'm sure it's something else'
'Mmmm'
'... I might get him a wee pressie'
'That's a good idea'
'Not clothes ... I got him that pink shirt on Valentine's Day'
'Yes, I remember'
'Some little thing that he'd like. I thought I'd cook a nice supper too, you know, make a bit of a fuss ... take his mind off things'
'... cufflinks?'

'She's been really down lately'
'Uh huh'
'I think things are a bit tricky at the office. I'm quite worried about her'
'Right'
'Last night she was awake half the night. She said she had stomach pains but I'm sure it's something else'
'Mmmm'
'... I might get her a wee pressie'
'That's a good idea'
'Not clothes ... I got her that pink shirt on Valentine's Day'
'Yes, I remember'
'Some little thing that she'd like. I thought I'd cook a nice supper too, you know, make a bit of a fuss ... take her mind off things'
'... earrings?'

One of these conversations takes place several times, every minute of every day all over the world.

The other is entirely fictitious.

Women talk about men the same way that they talk about everything else, i.e. a lot.

> Women know *Details* about their best friends' men which would horrify these men.

Things a Woman Knows about Her Best Friend's Man

- His job
- How things are going with his job
- The names of several people he works with
- The names of several members of his family
- His hobbies
- How much time he spends on these hobbies
- What kind of food, clothes, movies he likes
- Some other things he likes
- Quite a lot about *his* best friend
- An awful lot about his ex-girlfriend

The Double Act stays friends despite the New Man but their cinema planning chats change a bit. They start to go like this:

'Oh yes let's ... Tom's away on Wednesday and Thursday.'

They decide to go on Thursday.

They decide to go to something that Tom doesn't want to see.

On Thursday, after the cinema, when the women have finished their cappuccinos, and agreed about the cufflinks and had a hug, one of them hurries home. She is hoping that He called.

The other woman doesn't have quite such a spring in her step. Later, when she is getting ready for bed, she notices a few new kilos. As she lies in the dark, listening to nothing but the tick tock of the alarm clock, two thoughts are running simultaneously through her head.

One is: 'I am really glad that things are going so much better for Kate.'

The other is: '*All* my friends are going to Get Married and Go Away and I am *never* going to meet a man *ever* and I am going to be Hideously Lonely every weekend for the rest of my life.'

When a woman with a New Man arrives home to find the answering machine blinking a cheery hello, she is not too interested in the message from her mother. The instant she hears the second voice, though, she is just filled to the brim with fuzzy love. The woman replays the tape a couple of times, sighs and climbs the stairs. She slaps on all the new Nano-Zanospheres that she's bought in the past few weeks and she marvels at how much weight she seems to have lost without even trying. Life looks lovely. The woman is all overwhelmed with sharing and caring. She decides that it's awfully important to keep up with your chums, even when you've got a chap.

The very next Wednesday the woman with the New Man calls her chum and suggests a drink. After work. With the chap.

Once a woman has done a fair bit of Private Stuff with a New Man, she rather fancies doing a bit of Public Stuff ...

The chum, who has been saying: 'When am I going to meet this man then ...?' for weeks, agrees immediately. She's dead curious. She has built up an extremely detailed image of the New Man on account of all the things that she already knows about him.

When the woman arrives at the bar her friend is waiting. Alone. There's a slight nervy edge to her Sleek and Chic look. There's a slight nervy edge to her laugh. She isn't gassing on like she normally does because she keeps looking at the door to see whether anyone she knows is coming through it.

A man arrives who bears absolutely no resemblance whatsoever to Liam Neeson. One chum grins from ear to ear.

When a friend meets a New Man she knows the rules:
• Look nice
• Act friendly
• Smile indulgently whenever Private New Man Stuff is alluded to.

Both women feel a wee bit awkward with the addition of these rules into what was, previously, a pretty relaxed arrangement.

The man quite enjoys himself.

Later, one of the women asks her New Man what he thought of the friend. In an ideal New Man Meets Friend scenario the man says something like this: 'She's awfully nice and everything but not really fanciable.'

Then the woman says: 'Oh come on ... she's *gorgeous*' and grins from ear to ear.

It is not very hard to figure out what sort of circumstances apply in a worst case Friend Meets New Man scenario.

6

Oedipus Incredibly Complex

....

'Your father and I just want you to be happy, dear'

....

On Thursday morning one half of the Double Act figures she's going to be playing solo for a while. The weekend is stretching out, long and bleak, before her. She can't face it. She decides to have a couple of days at home.

A couple of days at home ...

On a Thursday afternoon when a cat and a flat looks like a lonely option, the idea of a couple of days at home seems rather cosy. Of course, if a few days with the folks was always such fun, the Samaritans wouldn't get so many calls over Christmas.

A woman isn't thinking about this when she dials her mother's number.

There are plenty of women who are chums with their mums.

There are the ones who lunch ... ('Wednesday then?').

There are the mummies who'll always be Mummy ... ('I'm cooking you some proper food, darling').

There are the daughters who are mummies ... ('Come on, Mummy, just *try* the soup').

Still, for lots of women the path doesn't run so smooth.

It starts when a woman is about fourteen. There is a shoe-shopping expedition. 'I am *not* wearing *those*.'

Mothers and daughters can go from nought to I Hate You in about four seconds under circumstances like these.

Some mothers and daughters never get out of the habit.

They roar right through the teen years.

'You are *not* wearing *that*.'

'I Hate You.'

Once the daughter is in her twenties the rage settles to a simmer. It only boils over occasionally. (Christmas tends to turn the heat up.)

After the woman has spoken to her mother she dials her friend's work number. The two of them have a bit of a gas about the New Man.

The friend says: 'He seems really nice.' (She says this even if she can conjure a detailed image of her friend phoning the Samaritans in six months' time.)

The woman with the New Man says they're off to Wales for the weekend. She is relieved when her possibly lonely pal tells her that she is going home for a couple of days.

The woman with the New Man says: 'That'll be nice.' (She says this even if the thought of going home for forty-five minutes sends her scrabbling for the Samaritans' number.)

The woman's mother picks her up at the train station. They have a hug. Just as they are about to get into the car the Mother makes a teeny tiny comment about the woman's shoes ...

The woman swallows hard.

Mentally, she congratulates herself. Afterwards she will say to a friend: 'I just don't let her *get* to me any more.'

Women who are not chums with their mums chat about this fact a fair bit. In the course of these chats the word 'Martyr' pops up more than frequently.

During supper the woman gets a bit of a grilling about how things are going. Fathers in these situations tend to have pretty much of a non-speaking part. Fathers in these situations tend to smile indulgently when the daughter says: 'Fine.'

Mothers are more suspicious. Luckily for daughters, mothers always have a friend with a daughter for whom things are going spectacularly well. The mother gives up on the grilling in order to relate all the *Details*, and then some, about her friend's daughter's going-spectacularly-wellness.

The father catches his daughter's eye and smiles indulgently. The daughter is rather enjoying her meat and two veg. The atmosphere is fairly relaxed.

When the mother finishes the story and sighs a teeny tiny sigh, and makes a teeny tiny comment about her own daughter's *not*-going-particularly-wellness, the daughter swallows hard.

Or: she throws the water jug.

Later that night, when the woman is lying in her old single bed, listening to nothing but the tick tock of the hallway clock, her mother is upstairs thinking '*all* her friends are going to Get Married and Go Away and she is *never* going to meet a man *ever* and she is going to be Hideously Lonely every weekend for the rest of her life ... if she doesn't do something about the state of her clothes/hair/friends/flat ...'

Sometimes a mother says something like this to a father.

A father tends to realise that it's best to stick pretty much with the non-speaking part in these situations.

When a woman is in going-well mode, even the most menacing mother is merely an irritant.

When a woman is in not-going-well mode, a mildly irritating mother grows horns.

Sometimes a woman just cannot deal with her mother any more so she goes out and gets herself another one.

Adopt-a-Mum is prevalent amongst teen girls. A girl takes a fancy to a friend's mother and makes her her own. The Adopt-a-Mum is a real chum.

'Your Mum is *so* much easier to talk to than mine,' says the girl. (The daughter can't always see it.)

Relationships like this can carry on well into adulthood.

When a woman whose Mum has been adopted, goes home for a couple of days, she has to be prepared for a good grilling re Kate's going-well status, as well as her own.

The mummy who will always be Mummy is a good candidate for an Adopt-a-Mum role. ('I bet you girls *never* eat any proper food.') So is the All Girls Together Gal.

The All Girls Together Gal dresses young for her age. She doesn't think of herself as a mum, she thinks of herself as one of the chums. Her daughter's friends think she's a gas. (The daughter can't always see it.)

This mother likes to wear her daughter's clothes. ('I can't believe your mother wears over-the-knee boots') and go where her daughter goes, and meet the men her daughter meets ...

It isn't hard to imagine a worst case All Girls Together Gal meets daughter's New Man scenario.

Mostly, though, mums chart a middle course.

A daughter and a mum go into the kitchen and pal around a bit, and do the dishes, and have a bit of a general gas and then, the mother says: 'I do wish your sister would do something about the state of her clothes/hair/friends/flat ...'

7

Kin Deep

....

'I did not say you could borrow it'

....

Some chums are chosen. Others are thrust upon us.

Lots of women have sisters.

One night, when two sisters are small, small girls, their mother leaves them somewhere strange. She kisses them goodbye. She smells all perfumey.

She says: 'Mummy won't be long. Be good for Mrs ... ' and she leaves.

At that moment the small, small girl children feel an intense love and need for each other. They soon forget all about it.

Later that night, when the sisters are lying in a strange double bed, listening to the tick tock of an unfamiliar hallway clock, one of them tries to get to sleep. One of them pretends to.

This is what happens next:

The Pretending one rolls, in an annoying way, towards the one who is Trying.

Then: The Pretending one flops her arm, in an *extremely* annoying way, over the Trying one.

The Trying one gives the Pretending one a shove.

The Pretending one repeats the procedure.
The Trying one hisses:
'Stop it'
Ditto.
'Stop it'
'What?'
Thump.
Wail.
Nought to Fight. Four Moves.

Suddenly the door opens. The light comes on. The hallway clock booms.

Mrs is standing in the doorway, disapproving. At that moment the small, small girl children feel an intense love and need for each other.

This pattern has a funny way of repeating itself throughout their lives.

PHASES IN SISTERHOOD

0-10:	Physical Violence. (Relieved by periods of unity in the face of adversity)
10-20:	Fierce Competitiveness. (Relieved by periods of Physical Violence)
20-30:	Slow Dawning of New Respect. (Interrupted by periods of Fierce Competitiveness)
30-plus:	Slow Dawning of Genuine Friendship

Sometimes a woman has a sister for whom going-well isn't so much a phase as a condition. In cases like these the mother doesn't bother with dragging up the daughter of a friend to rant on about over supper. In cases like these a not-going-well woman is likely to feel her hand twitching toward the water jug before she's touched her meat and two veg.

Mostly, though, sisters chart a middle course.

Once women have licked the Nought to Fight thing (except

at Christmas, and that doesn't count) they tend to develop a special sort of chumship with their sisters. The difference between sisters and other sorts of best friends is that a woman forgives her sister much less than she would a chum, on a day-to-day level. ('I've never been able to stand the way you do that.')

On the major big deal level she forgives her everything. This is because a woman knows that when the chips are down and things are going absolutely-bloody-terribly a sister will be there.

When a woman in her thirties finds out her sister has got Real Trouble all the bad stuff that has gone before is forgotten.

Bad Stuff that has Gone Before ...

- Damn near killing each other
- Scarring the other one for life ('It was an accident')
- Spilling the beans on each other. ('She did it on purpose')
- Siding with a mother against the other one
- Flirting with the other one's bloke

The women can forget and forgive all this because of the bonding stuff that has gone before.

Bonding Stuff that has Gone Before ...

- Secrets
- Sucking water off flannels
- Damn near killing some other girl (possibly scarring her for life)
- Backing each other up to the hilt (in the row that followed the other-girl episode)
- Siding with each other against a common foe (a mother/that other girl)
- Getting rid of the other one's bloke for her ('No, she's definitely gone out')

When the woman gets back from her couple of days at home she calls her sister.

The sister says: 'I was just thinking about you.'

When a woman in her thirties finds out her sister has got Real Trouble, she says, 'I knew something was wrong.' Quite often, she did.

The woman gives her sister a blow-by-blow account of the mother's friend's daughter's going-spectacularly-wellness. They both make moaning noises and laugh like drains.

The woman tells her sister *all* about Kate's New Man.

They have a bit of a forty-five minute session.

The woman sighs and says to her sister: 'Sometimes I worry that *all* my friends are going to Get Married and Go Away and I am *never* going to meet a man *ever* ...'

If the woman's sister has A Man, she immediately starts a mental trawl of his filofax. If she hasn't she says: 'Ooh I know, me too.'

Either way the conversation ends on an encouraging note.

The women say good night. They think: 'Sisters are the *best*.'

They think: 'It's lovely to have chums, but you can tell a sister anything.'

The woman who has been home for a couple of days has *not* told her sister that their mother gave her Granny's gold bracelet just as she was getting ready to go for the train.

The sister will find out.

When she does she will say: 'I can't *believe* she gave you that bracelet.'

'What?' the other woman will say, pretending. 'I was *promised* that bracelet.'

'When?'

Four ... Three ... Two ...

8

Pick 'n' Mix

....

'Kath's the sexy one, Mandy's the clever one, and I'm the nice one'

....

When a woman has had a bit of a mini-barney with her sister ... ('Honestly, it's just a bracelet') and is finding her mother's phone calls a teeny bit irritating ('Does she think I can *remember* these people?') and her best friend is all tied up with some chap ('She can't talk about anything else'), she could start to feel kind of friendless.

But, just as a detailed image of every weekend for the rest of her life flashes in front of her, the phone rings. It's one of the Pasta Party set.

The women have a good gas. They haven't seen each other for ages so there's a fair bit of catching up to do ...

'She can't talk about anything else.'

The phoning pal explains that her New Man is now Old News. They decide to go to the cinema.

The good thing about the Pasta Party set, the Gang, the Crowd, is that circumstances are constantly changing. This gives women some flexibility on the Double Act front.

A woman's circle of friends tend to overlap at the edges. They don't always know each other. (Usually they know a fair bit *about* each other.) But, if she were to assemble the Full Set, including sisters, Thursday Nighters, ex-Double Acts, and the minor-birthday-celebration bunch, a woman would probably find she'd collected one or two of the following ...

The It Girl

This is the woman who *always* has a great haircut, a fabulous monochrome outfit and Man (often New). She's a bit wearing (the others gain a kilo and snag their tights just from being in the room with her) but she gives the crowd a certain pzazz.

The women have a sort of love-hate crush on her. They cannot decide whether they are irritated or relieved that she shows no interest whatsoever in their men. (These men are under strict surveillance whenever she is around.)

The Intensely Irritating One

Quite often there's a woman in a group who gets right up the noses of several of the others. She makes terrific forty-five-minute fodder on account of the fact that they can convince themselves that ferocious bitching about her isn't really evil, wicked, shrewishness because, after all, *everybody* feels the same way.

The Sweet One

Doesn't bitch. She never forgets birthdays. She has a tendency to give people things that are home made. She's got good skin and she *could* be *really* pretty. The Sweet One gets a teeny bit ignored. The other women are absolutely stunned when she shows up with some complete dish one Christmas Eve and marries him on Valentine's Day.

The We've Known Each Other For Years Friend

Shares a woman's history. These two may no longer have much in common but the fact that they remember each other's first car/gym teacher/boss, serves as a tie to bind them. Sometimes when they are chatting to a newer chum, they sigh and say: 'I don't really know why we're still friends', but then they get together and have a right laugh about their first husbands.

Miss Madly Bad

Lives on the edge. She can show a gal a thing or two. Often these things have to do with illegal substances. (Teen Madly Bads show another girl how to stick her fingers down her throat after lunch.) Miss Madly Bad's appeal tends to wane once she's tapped everyone for loans, got into some deep trouble with a series of New Man rat-bags, slept on everybody's sofas and damn near killed herself.

A Late Bloomer

One of these can really ruffle the rest of the crowd. She goes along like one of the bunch for absolutely ever and then she suddenly starts her own business/becomes a successful painter/leaves her husband/loses two stone and moves to Paris.

Women Who Don't Make The Team (But Sneak in Anyhow)

Man Stealers.

Nowadays nobody cuts anyone off for stealing an outside girl's man but those in the inner circle are sacred.

Mostly, in real life, these characters don't come out quite so whole as they do in Hollywood. The M1 isn't exactly teeming with Sweet Ones who've ditched their kids for four thrill-filled days in a Dodge with a dangerous-to-know pal.

Mostly, in real life, women know lots of watered-down versions of the above. Also, women play most of the parts at some point.

Even the most irritating sister can have a circle of chums who think she's It.

A woman is all the women she is on account of being a natural born actress. Also, there's the Chameleon Effect.

Not a lot about a woman is set in stone. (Men have an inkling of this.)

Women are not averse to a bit of a change. (The fashion industry has more than an inkling of this.)

Women are often quite easily influenced as to the sort of change they'll make. (The advertising industry is cleaning up.)

But, a woman doesn't just scan ads and mags for transformation tips. A woman relies on the other girls. Sometimes the changes she makes go beyond the superficial.

The Chameleon Effect is at its most powerful when a woman has a New Best Friend.

New Best Friends

occasionally appear in the life of one of the group.

The New Best Friend is awfully influential. Matching over-the-knee boots may ensue. (An increased interest in the environment isn't out of the question.) The woman who has got a New Best Friend quotes her ... *ad nauseam.*

The others say: 'Who *is* this Hilary, anyhow?'

Often these friendships last for a few months and then peter out. The woman slinks back to the fold and nobody says any more about it.

The fledgling Double Act meets up outside the cinema.

One of the women holds the handbags while the other one squishes in for popcorn. When they sit down they have a bit of a gas. They discover that they both love that actress who always plays the dangerous-to-know one.

As the lights fade, they feel a wee wave of pleasure. It's to do with having someone to share and care with.

9

Let's Spend the Week Together

···

'Don't look ... Don't look ... it's those two jerks from the beach, they're at the bar.

Oh no, they're coming over. Don't look'

···

Sometimes, when women are sitting in the cinema wearing their comfy shoes (unwashed hair, unshaven legs), sharing a pot of popcorn, an ad for Bacardi comes on. Lots of people who do not look as though they own a pair of comfy shoes are having fun in the sun on the silver screen.

The women are suddenly very aware of their extra bits of bottom. They sigh.

Later, over a cappuccino, one of the women says:

'I really fancy a break,'

and the other one says:

'Ooh, me too.'

These women decide to go on holiday. Together. They say: 'I don't care where we go, as long as it's Somewhere Sunny.'

They imagine that when they get Somewhere Sunny they will look like Demi Moore.

THINGS WOMEN SAY WHEN THEY ARE ABOUT TO GO ON HOLIDAY TOGETHER

- 'I'm taking two swimsuits, one sarong and a t-shirt ... and maybe, a dress for the evening. That's it.'
- 'Fruit and fish. Fruit and fish. That is *all* I want to eat ... nothing but really, really healthy food.'
- 'We're going to have an *amazing* time.'

THINGS WOMEN DO WHEN THEY ARE ABOUT TO GO ON HOLIDAY TOGETHER

Go to Boots and spend about £45. (Everyone knows that you need a *new* hand cream to take on holiday.) Also, there's the exfoliating mitt. Buy several small, zip-up thingies which would be ideal for packing tights ... or something ... in. Buy a fabulously useful black holiday frock (as recommended by *Elle*) and maybe just a couple of t-shirts ... nothing much. Buy some gold sandals. Buy a white shirt (*needed* anyway so it doesn't count). Get a haircut. Buy this *fantastic* product which protects hair from the effects of sun and sea. Go on a sunbed. Plaster fake tan all over the sunbedded body (after using the exfoliating mitt). Use an incredible variety of hair-removing potions. Pack an incredible variety of hair-removing potions. Check on the Demi Moore look-alike progress. Decide that a kilo or three and the new Nano-Zanosphere Complex will make all the difference. Find out the price of the new Nano-Zanosphere Complex. Decide to buy it at the Duty Free. Talk to each other every night on the phone ... for ages. Say: 'We're going to have an *amazing* time' at the end of every one of these conversations.

When they leave ...

the women are *very* excited. It doesn't matter how old they are, they feel about sixteen. They act about sixteen on the way to the airport. When they get to the airport they have an absolute ball in the duty-free shops and then they buy about fifteen magazines, some peppermints and some more hand cream. They are almost goose bumpy with pleasure by the time they board the plane.

When they arrive ...

it's Sunny. The women feel very high-spirited indeed. They keep feeling like this until the mini coach, which is going to their hotel, has been driving for forty minutes through unrelieved, barren scrubland. They don't perk up again 'til much later, when they've walked down to the beach.

When they see the sea ...

and stand on the sand, and feel the gentle late afternoon breeze on their skin they feel much better. They forget all about the plastic mattress covers and decide to go back and Get Changed and have a drink in the bar.

Getting Changed is a major feature of women on holiday. Women on holiday Get Changed just as often as they would if they were on holiday with a man.

The Getting Changed part is much more fun minus-a-man, on account of not being rushed, and not having to worry about what they look like with wet hair. The new clothes help too.

When they have got changed, the women say: 'You look nice' to each other and they go down to the bar. All of a sudden, deep in their collective subconscious this little, unbidden thought occurs: 'I wish I were with a Man.'

The women don't say this, they say things like: 'It's much less hassle going on holiday without a man' instead.

On the first day: the women wake up early. They have a Healthy breakfast. They decide that the cloud is bound to lift soon and they may as well head for the beach.

> When women go on holiday together they go with someone who looks pretty much the same as they do in a bathing suit. (If one of them looks really spectacular in a bathing suit and the other one doesn't, it is because the other one tans brilliantly and has got gorgeous hair.)

When the women have made it to the beach (they had a shufti in the shops on the way on account of the clouds not lifting as smartly as they'd hoped), and got rid of some geezer flogging sarongs, and agreed *not* to set up next to those other girls (brilliant tans and gorgeous hair), they slap on their Fun in the Sun Nano-Zanospheres and get their books out.

They don't get much reading done, though, because they're doing too much gassing. The cloud lifts. Life looks lovely.

Much, much later they decide that it's time to go back and Get Changed.

They decide that they're pretty done-in from so much Fun in the Sun.

They decide not to bother with dressing all-out Sleek and Chic.

They decide they'll leave trekking down to that pasta place on the other side of town 'til another day.

They decide to have a fairly early night.

This pattern repeats itself for several days. With variations ...

On one of the days the women Get Changed into *each other's* clothes.

On one of the days the women cave and have waffles for breakfast. (It doesn't matter which day this happens on, it sets a precedent for the rest of the holiday.)

On one of the days the women discover that their conversation has gone full circle like a Muzak recording, and they both get stuck into their books.

On the fifth day: one of the women wants to go back to that shop they saw on the first day. (She spotted something there which would go with something she's already got.) She wants to do this straight after they've had their waffles. The other woman mentions that the morning is showing promise, cloud-lifting wise, and *she* fancies a change of beach scene, which necessitates an early start.

A bit of a forty-five minuter ensues. The women state their own cases over and over like a Muzak recording. Things get tense. Voices get clipped. The women decide to go their separate ways.

They tug on their espadrilles and set off in opposite directions. They are both in a bit of a huff. They both think: 'I wish I were with a Man.'

Later, the women meet up. They are a bit subdued. They decide to have a mineral water. They ask each other how they got on. There is a slight nervy edge to their enquiries. They are sipping in silence when some absolute trollop (brilliant tan, gorgeous hair) walks into the bar wearing a string bikini and a smile.

The women roll their eyes at each other. They say: 'Who *does* she think she is?' and laugh.

That night they get Sleeked and Chiced up to the absolute nines and hit the pasta place. They have an *amazing* time.

When women come back from an *amazing* holiday there is always a song which reminds them of it. Whenever they hear this song they say: 'This song always reminds me of our holiday. We had such an *amazing* time.'

They say this *ad nauseam*.

10

Toil and Trouble

A woman isn't always able to convince her mother that she has a serious job.

When a woman gets back from Somewhere Sunny it doesn't seem like two minutes since she was ducking out of the office to buy the fabulously useful black holiday frock. (This frock has had two wearings. One by each woman.)

On Monday morning, when her feet hit the pavement wearing something other than espadrilles, she feels a bit blue. But she is buoyed right up again when she gets to work and the other girls tell her how fab her tan looks.

At some point during the day one of these girls will duck out for a cappuccino with her so as to catch up on all the *Details*.

Lots of women make friends at work.

WORK MATES

Have lunch together
  Are united against a common foe (the boss/some other woman who is Intensely Irritating)
  Know all the *Details* about each other's men, mothers, friends and frock purchases.
  Often, they have never set foot in each other's homes. Sometimes, though, this barrier is crossed. Women work mates who graduate to sofa-level familiarity can remain friends for life.

Unless ...

When women are young, and new to cut and thrust, it's awfully easy to pal around. They have a lot of laughs at the expense of Swotty-bossy types who *never* come in looking like they've had a weekend on the town.

One day, two young work mates are having a bit of a gas (one of them spotted a frock, in a shop, on the way to work and is wondering whether it will go with something she's already got). This conversation is interrupted when a Swotty-bossy type pops her head over the partition, which separates their desks from the hallway bit, and asks one of the work mates whether she's free for lunch.
  The work mate says yes. (She sounds a bit surprised.) The Swotty-bossy type retreats to her office and the work mates roll their eyes at each other.
  At lunch time one woman looks at a frock while the other one lunches with the Swotty-bossy type.
  The woman who is looking at the frock decides that it will be fabulously useful. The woman who is lunching with the Swotty-bossy type decides not to order something piggy.

Conversation at lunch is a bit stilted. The Swotty-bossy type makes most of the running. Eventually, she puts down her glass of mineral water and offers the young work mate a promotion. The young work mate is thrilled. She says so.

The Swotty-bossy type fills her in on *all* the *Details*. The conversation picks up some pace. A bit of a gas ensues. The young work mate decides that the Swotty-bossy type isn't so Swotty or bossy after all.

During the afternoon the woman who shopped stops by the desk of the woman who lunched. She wants to show her the frock. While she is wrestling with tissue paper and mentioning a few things she's already got, she asks what happened at lunch. (She sounds casual.)

The woman-with-a-promotion tells her work mate what happened at lunch. She sounds vague. She leaves out a lot of the *Details*.

If a woman stops coming into work looking like she's had a weekend on the town, while her pal is still dragging herself to her desk in a decidedly unSleek and Chic state, the friendship might wane.

Unless ...

Sometimes a woman gets a taste for promotion. She starts dragging herself to her desk at dawn. She is fanatical about *Details* She gives up on frock shops altogether.

One day, this woman has been at her desk for several hours when another woman, who has not yet removed her coat, pops her head around her office door. 'Kate's birthday today.' she says, 'Lunch at Pellinis.'

Coat woman repeats this procedure at the next office. This is the office of a Man who has had roughly the same number of promotions as his neighbour.

This Man does not:

a) Worry that he should have ordered flowers for Kate.
b) Wonder whether he ought to pop out and get Kate a little something.
c) Try to reorganise his day so that he can make lunch at Pellini's.

Reasons a woman-with-promotions might immediately do all of the above under these circumstances ...

She is absolutely desperate not to be thought of as a Swottybossy type.

A woman who runs her own show is perfectly capable of shelling out for two dozen over-priced roses and lunch for the entire staff because it is the birthday of an utterly useless assistant who hasn't pitched up on time for months.

> Most women want to be One Of The Girls even when they're way up there whipping the arses of the Men.

One morning, early, the woman-with-promotions is having a meeting with some other promoted people. They decide that they're going to have to *do something* about an utterly useless assistant who hasn't pitched up on time for months. They agree that a dressing-down would be a good start. They discuss who ought to administer it. The woman-with-promotions draws the short straw.

That afternoon she pops her head over a partition outside her office and asks one of the women sitting there whether she's got a minute. The woman who is sitting there says yes. The woman-with-promotions goes back into her office and waits. Over the partition a bit of eye-rolling is going on.

Eventually, the utterly useless assistant sticks her head round the office door. She is waved in. A dressing-down is administered. She leaves.

Not much later the woman-with-promotions goes to the loo. When she passes the partition an upset assistant is being comforted by two work mates (also unpromoted) and words to the effect of Swotty-bossy type are being bandied about.

The woman-with-promotions feels a bit miserable. On the way to the loo she wonders how she can become One Of The Girls again. When she comes out of the cubicle she gives her hair a half-hearted pat. She sighs. Suddenly this little unbidden thought pops out of her subconscious: 'I have worked hard to get where I am and people are just going to have to *accept* that I'm the Boss.'

She feels better. She strides past the partition with her head held high. Dagger looks hit her back. Doubts rise up to prick her.

Quite often, a woman-with-promotions finds that these two reactions alternate with gathering intensity. Eventually her office behaviour is swinging wildly from Wimpy One of the Girls to complete Swotty-bossy bitch quicker than you can say, 'Lunch is on me.'

Other people end up having a meeting to decide what to do about *her.*

A woman doesn't just worry about the effect that career success might have on her work mates. There are her other chums too.

A woman worries that the day her desk distracts her for long enough to forget to phone a friend, is the day the other women will say: 'She's not the same since she had that promotion.'

A woman is not always way off the mark with this particular concern.

Sometimes one of the women will utter the not-the-same line way before a phone call is ever forgotten. Five'll get ya ten this woman is:

a) in a serious not-going-well state,

or

b) a previously perfectly OK individual who has been friends with the promoted woman for absolutely ever and works in a similar industry with not a promotion in sight.

This is not the only line women have in their promotion-put-down arsenal. There's another one: 'Men don't like successful women, do they?'

Women don't even have to say this, they simply imply it: 'Well, I mean she's at her desk from dawn 'til dark.'

A woman can be as subtle as she wants on this tack. Another woman will usually pick up the thread. That's because, secretly, lots of women suspect that it's true.

One Thursday night a woman who has been hovering over her desk from dawn 'til dark stops in to search for something edible at the Eight 'til Late.

Suddenly a cat and a flat look like a lonely option. A wee nagging thought occurs in her head. It's this: 'If I keep putting *all* my energy into my career I am *never* going to meet a Man *ever* and I am going to be Hideously Lonely every weekend for the rest of my life ...'

Later, when she has finished the pre-packed pasta, this woman decides to take a couple of weeks off and go Somewhere Sunny. She calls a chum who has the kind of attitude to work which means that she is constantly keen to take a couple of weeks off and go Somewhere Sunny. They have a good old gas. During this conversation the promoted woman's chum reminds her that there's more to life than work.

The next day the promoted woman pops out at lunchtime and buys herself a fabulously useful black holiday frock.

11

Situations Vacant

....

'Do you fancy giving up work, taking up yoga, having weekly facials, and doing lots and lots of shoe shopping?'

Many women dream that, some day, a fairy godmother will say something like this to them.
     The Fairy Godmother in question is a man.

....

In 1909 Helen Rowland wrote:
'When you see what some girls marry, you realize how they must hate to work for a living.'

Things have changed since 1909. These are the things:
     One: Marriage is no longer a reason to stop working.
     Two: Nobody has the nerve to say stuff like this any more.

Many women have a schizoid approach to the career thing.

There is one face, that they show to men, and women with whom they are competing, and another face that they show to their friends.

Rather a lot more women than will ever admit it decide, round the upper-mid-level promotion mark, that the levels above them look decidedly like Lonely Weekend country. These women begin to tread water. Treading water gets tiring.

A woman who has been treading water for a while finds her feet dragging on the way to her corner office. This woman begins to fantasise about a life in which she wouldn't have to save up bonuses and due days before she could pop off Somewhere Sunny. This woman begins to fantasise about being kept.

Rather a lot more women than will ever admit it share this fantasy.

One night, two women who've cheered on each other's approach to the upper-mid-level promotion mark are sitting on a sofa. The wine bottle next to them is open, and then some. They have a bit of a gas about the rest of the gang. Then one of them mentions that work has been getting her down. She says she feels that all she does these days is hover over a desk from dawn 'til dark. She says she feels as though she's going to be doing this for the rest of her life.

The other one sighs and says: 'Ooh, me too.'

The women finish their wine. One of them gets up to go to the loo and the other one starts making coffee in a half-hearted sort of way. When they are both settled back on the sofa, one says: 'I can't imagine *not* working, can you?'

'Uuh, uuh.'

'I'd *never* give up work.'
'*Never.*'
'Ideally I'd like something ... part time.'
'Perfect.'

Women know that working part time will barely pay for a cat, let alone a flat. That's where being kept comes in.

Not a lot of women want to be kept like an Old-Fashioned Mistress.

Women who *do* want to be kept like an Old-Fashioned Mistress don't bother with facades. They bleach the hell out of their hair from age seventeen and advertise their intentions anywhere that they might get noticed.

Women within this club don't make friends with each other much beyond the lending-the-hairspray level.

A lot of women want to be kept like a Modern Wife.

THE KEPT MODERN WIFE CLUB

Habitat: Grander than a flat
Habits: Lunch (lots of shopping afterwards)
Hobbies: Something that she might, eventually, make a business
             of ... part time.

Women who make it to the Kept Modern Wife Club sometimes feel a bit guilty, no matter how much they tell themselves and each other that this is the life they deserve.

One of the reasons that a Kept Modern Wife might, sometimes, feel just a teensy weensy bit guilty if she were really pressed, is the fact that she shoved some other woman right off her perch in order to get to this position.

This woman is the Second Kept Modern Wife. She has a lonely life.

This is why ... A woman who snatches a chap out of someone else's hands has usually heard this expression: 'What goes round, comes round.'

She secretly suspects that it's true. This gal doesn't trust other women as far as she can shove 'em. She sure as hell doesn't trust her man. She daren't loosen her grasp for a second. She soon discovers that following a fellow from go to woe and filling her days with endless shopping is *not* the stuff of dreams.

Kept Modern Wives tend to lose touch with those members of the set who are:

> Still Single
> Still Broke

It is a rare Kept Modern Wife Club member who sets a dinner party table for five.

The Kept Modern Wife doesn't lose contact with all her old friends immediately.

At first she wants her old friends in the club with her. So, she trawls her husband's filofax and introduces all the ones who are:

> Still Single
> Still Broke

to those friends (and some pretty distant acquaintances, actually) of her husband's who are:

> Still Single
> Not at All Broke.

If the old friends simply refuse to make the best of these marvellous opportunities ('And, God knows, I've *tried*') the Kept Modern Wife gives up. This giving up is done with more than a note of exasperation if a sister is involved.

Then she gets on with it.

One day a Kept Modern Wife shakes her perfectly coiffed head and says to another Kept Modern Wife over lunch: 'Can you believe that Kate is *still* working there ...?'

But a Kept Modern Wife tends to forget something when she first signs up for the club's full benefits. It is this: If you're going to be Kept, you're going to have a Keeper.

The Kept Modern Wife realises this on the day that she bumps into one of the old crowd who is:

Still Single
Going Bloody Well (wherever she wants to).

12

Absolutely Fad-ulous

....

'So, what are we doing today? uh-huh ... mmmmmm. Weeeell, I think we should consider the texture, maybe go with the curl ... yes? ... keep the weight on top, but break it up a bit, just here ... you see? that way we'll get some movement, and then we can just soften the hairline like ... this, but, still keep it sharp at the nape ... so as to avoid the messy stage. With me? Goood.'

....

When a woman conjures a detailed image of herself working part time (just after she's set the alarm for 7 am Monday) she leaves out lying in late and watching telly in the mornings.

A woman imagines herself working part time and pursuing all her other Interests.

When a woman is a girl child there is a day on which she Simply Must have a skipping rope with stripey handles.

Simply Musts are a big feature of the lives of girl children (and their mothers).

Simply Musts are invoked over things as diverse as tap lessons, bedroom furnishings and pierced ears.

The reason for girls' Simply Musts is: *everyone* else is doing it.

Crazes are a girl thing. Boys do have them. Under six they do dinosaurs and cowboys and, in their teens, clothes and haircuts can be a bit of an issue, but by then they've usually discovered Man United, so they're pretty well set up. Interest wise, for the rest of their lives.

Girls actually say, 'I'll just *die* if I have to wear that.' Girls actually believe this. (Lots of mothers pretend that they've never heard anything so silly.)

Girls do not grow out of this stuff.

The fashion, diet and magazine industries are reliant on this fact. Home improvement companies, the advertising business and publishers are beneficiaries of the knock-on effects.

In fact, if all women stopped talking to each other for a month a lot of people would go broke. Nobody is very worried about this possibility.

A Craze is not a hobby. A hobby is an ongoing, developing thing. A Craze is something which disappears just as suddenly as it appears.

SIGNS OF A NEW CRAZE

- Sudden onset of wallpaper stripping
- Sudden appearance of large bag full of needles, wool and other paraphernalia in the sitting room
- Complete overhaul of the contents of the fridge
- Two large sacks in the hallway labelled Oxfam
- Bedside copy of any book with the words 'A New Approach to' in the title. (The name of the author of this book is likely to start popping up in conversation as if she were a family friend.)

As women get older they are a teeny bit less prone to across-the-board Crazes.

When grown-up married women with kids see three young things struggling along in matching clogs they say: 'How funny ... remember when we did that' and laugh.

These same women are able to convince themselves, each other, and possibly their husbands that they Simply Must have Tinkerbell themed invitations for their daughter's first birthday party because that is what one-year-olds like.

When a Craze first starts a woman has conversations like this with her friends:

'I've been thinking about redoing the spare room.'

'Really?'

'Mmm. I thought I might colour wash it.'

'Oooh, right.'

or

'I think this gluten free thing *really* is the answer.'

'.'.. do you?'

Craze-catching is complicated by the fact that there is an unwritten law in woman-land that you *cannot* just go out and buy the exact same outfit/wallpaper/earrings or Top to Toe Stretch 'n' Tone Course as another woman unless you are actually with her on the expedition to purchase. (In which case it's your duty to encourage her by spending your own gas money too.)

If the Irritating One does this she provides the others with forty-five minute fodder for a week. They say: 'I couldn't *believe* it. It was *exactly* the same ... well, in the blue, which isn't nearly as nice ... but exactly the same otherwise ...'

This means that women have to Craze-catch in a roundabout sort of way (which is pretty much how they do most things). They do this:

When the friend mentions Stencilling/Tapestry/Lactose Intolerance or AHAs the other woman says something like: 'Ooooh yes, I read/heard/saw something about that in *Good Housekeeping*/on The Clothes Show/at the gym ... what do you think?' (This way she has made it clear that she'd be quite interested in giving it a whirl as well.)

They discuss *all* the *Details* for about forty-five minutes.

They are absolute experts by the time they casually mention it to some other woman.

There is one particularly common New Craze heralding phrase in woman-land. It's this: 'What do you think about a fringe?'

This question requires absolutely no introductory conversational gambit. Another woman can always pick up the thread.

It is a corny and old-fashioned notion that women spend hours and·hours thinking about and talking about their hair.

It is a corny and old-fashioned notion that women change their hair as a way of improving their mood/relieving boredom/altering their lives.

It is an absolute one hundred percent fact.

Women don't allow lack of cash to keep their New Hair hopes down. If they can't afford a poncy hairdresser, they make do with a cheap one. If they can't manage that, they buy a few make-and-do packs and gadgets from Boots. (Quite often, they do all three, much to the disdain of the poncy hairdresser.)

One Thursday night a woman who has been treading water for a while with no part time possibilities whatever on the horizon, mentions the new fringe to an old chum. As she speaks, she pulls her Trying-On Face and tugs a handful of her hair into a daft loopy arrangement on her forehead.

The friend can't quite see it.

'Anyway,' she says, 'you've got *gorgeous* hair.'

A bit of a forty-five minuter ensues. The phrase 'fed up' is uttered more than frequently.

By the end of this conversation the woman has decided that she Simply Must have her fringe cut. *Now.* (*Now* is a major New Craze feature.)

The friend goes to the loo. When she gets back she finds the woman sitting in the kitchen with a tea-towel around her neck. She is gleefully brandishing a pair of blunt scissors.

If the women have finished their wine, the convincing doesn't take forty-five minutes.

The hacker starts out timidly. The phrase 'keep still' pops up. A lot.

Eventually, the hackee races off to the bathroom to check on the Demi Moore look-alike progress.

It is quite likely that one of these women will have the worst weekend she's had for quite a while.

13

Flotsam and Then Some

....

'And I'll tell you how I know. I know because she goes to the same osteopath as me'

....

A woman who's learnt her lesson with regard to fringe trimming, can get quite friendly with her hairdresser. In fact, the pursuit of Crazes introduces a woman to lots of new folks.

There's …

The Club Chum

This relationship is particularly prevalent at gyms. The women see each other every Tuesday. They have a bit of a gas while they're changing for aerobics. Sometimes they have a mineral water together afterwards. By the time they've caved and started ordering cappuccinos they know each other's Man Status and a fair bit about each other's Work Status. Sometimes they know roughly where the other one lives. Mostly, though, they say stuff like this: 'I'm sure she's giving us more abdominals than she used to.'

The Aroma/Colour/Acu Therapist

When a woman like this comes into another woman's life it is usually via a chum.

'Honestly, she's just great ... you'll *feel* amazing.'

The woman has a good old gas with the Aroma/Colour/Acu Therapist about how amazing she *isn't* feeling. She mentions that work has been getting her down. The Aroma/Colour/Acu Therapist listens in a very caring way. Then she shares some of her Aroma/Colour/Acu wisdom with the woman. This has a bit of a New Best Friend effect.

'She's told me I must *never* wear navy.'

The Aroma/Colour/Acu Therapist lasts about as long as a New Best Friend. 'I get away from work so late these days I'm just too tired to trek all the way down there.'

X that I go to X with

Is a step up from the Club Chum. This is someone from the edge of the group with whom the woman has suddenly become firm friends due to a shared interest in Wine Tasting, Painting or Pastry Preparation. These women sign up for classes together and then trek halfway across town every Tuesday at 7 pm. On the way they have a bit of a gas and comparison of the essential equipment they've shelled out for since last week. On the way back one of them invites the other one in for coffee. She says, 'No, no, it's late.' Then the two of them sit in the car for forty-five minutes and talk. This friendship bites the dust with the onset of the first frost.

'My' Decorator

This is mostly a Modern Kept Wife sort of friendship. It is distinguished by the use of the personal pronoun. There's 'my' caterer too. Plus a few 'my' women-in-white-coats who are privy to just how much extra bottom the woman has got. Women in the Second Wife Club often have their most meaningful same-sex relationships with these people.

Women who are going-bloody-well get a crack at pals like this too, but mostly the going-bloody-well gal puts up with peeling paint, dines out and makes reluctant friends with 'my' accountant instead.

Sometimes a woman just forms a bit of a bond with the girl at the Whole-Healthy food store or the Beauty Shop Sherpa who remembers to hold back a bottle of Passion Fire for her: 'You Simply Must try it ...' But she usually builds up a wee collection of folks with whom she can have a gas without ever settling into a sofa.

The Never on a Sofa set isn't reliant on Crazes for growth.

There's also:

The Phone Friend

This is a working woman's relationship. The Phone Friend is often called Darling. She is commonly found in industries where lots of people get called Darling. A woman has a real rapport with her Phone Friend. Usually, they talk often. Usually, they never meet. They admire one another's working methods. When one of them leaves her job they say ... 'We *must* keep in touch.' Usually, they never speak again.

Sometimes a woman has a Phone Friend who is male. She is likely to admire his working methods too, but there is always a bit of underlying flirtation practice going on. Meeting for lunch is a possibility under these circumstances – usually this is courting disaster. Meeting for anything else is definitely courting disaster.

Friends of Friends

These are people who a woman does not physically know at all. In fact she could sit next to them on the No. 9 night bus and be none the wiser. But she knows *all* about them.

Women talk to each other about their friends. If these friends have not met, a woman feels that it's OK to really spill the beans about the other one. This doesn't count as gossiping because, the woman figures, their paths won't cross.

This little woman-logic code means that a woman knows that another woman's husband likes to dress up in said woman's nurse's uniform.

It's all fascinating, harmless fun until there's a house party in Wales and someone says: 'Sorry, *what* did you say your last name was again?'

Occasionally, a woman who gets home late a lot finds that her same-sex friendships have got to an awfully low ebb. There's only one other woman who ever gets near her sofa. Mostly, her relationship with this woman is conducted on paper. This paper tends to consist of old envelopes. These old envelope notes say: 'You need more bleach.'

One almost end-of-the week night, after aerobics, a woman gets home and starts to unpack her Eight 'til Late plastic sack before she's even taken her coat off. The phone rings when she's putting the bleach away. It's Kate.

'I was just thinking about you,' says the woman. (And she was.)

The women have a bit of a gas. Then Kate says: 'What are you up to next weekend?'

The woman conjures a detailed image of next weekend. It includes lying in late and watching telly in the mornings.

'Not *too* much ... Why?'

'We're going to Wales. Want to come?'

The woman knows who this 'we' refers to. A fellow who is absolutely nothing like Liam Neeson, but not a bad sort for all that, is included in it. Kate's New Man isn't so new any more.

The woman gives the bleach cupboard a shove with her foot. She thinks that a couple of days in the country might be quite nice.

She says: 'Oh ... all right then. Yes, I suppose I could.'

'Great', says Kate. She sounds very enthusiastic. 'Who else is going?' says the woman. She sounds a bit suspicious.

Kate names a Male/Female Double Act and one lone man. When pressed she gives the woman a few details about this man. They are fairly flattering.

The woman begins to sound a bit unsure. Kate says: 'Oh come on, it'll be fun and we haven't seen you for ages.' (And they haven't.)

The woman is convinced. Almost. She says OK. She hangs up and takes off her coat.

A wee, small, hopeful part of her brain starts to quite look forward to the weekend.

14

Two by Two

In addition to Crazes, women have Phases. A woman is always in some Phase or other.

The Phase she is in determines her susceptibility to certain Crazes. The Phase she is in determines which of the bunch she is day-to-day-really-good-chums with.

A woman may have a Best Friend who is in a different Phase altogether but she does not talk to this woman *every* day on the telephone.

The day-to-day-really-good-chum is someone who can sympathise about snagged tights/no promotion/cleaning woman/first birthday party incident. This means she almost definitely has a recent snagged tights/no promotion/cleaning woman/first birthday incident of her own to relate.

Here are some of the Phases women go through (in chronological order):

Working Girl	Clothes Phase
Men	Social Phase
Couple	House Phase
Children	No Time For Anything Else! Phase
Settled	How's Next Weekend For You? Phase

Sometimes Phases overlap: e.g. Working Girl and House
or occur singly: e.g. Baby minus Couple.

But, essentially, women consider that if this happens it isn't quite the Real Thing.

Quite late, on a Friday night, a woman arrives at a pub in Wales (looking more Sleek and Chic than she normally would for such an occasion). She sees her friends. They are sitting in the corner with one, lone male. A detailed image in the woman's head of herself (kind of Demi Moorish), and a Liam Neeson look-alike taking a cosy country walk, dissolves. There's a slight nervy edge to her smile when this man is introduced ... he's a Double Act half. A wee small, hopeful part of the woman's brain sighs and gets back into action.

Everybody has a bit of a gas. (The missing Double Act half is back from the loo.) The pub door opens. Kate's man grins from ear to ear. Everyone turns around. A lone man who looks like a really good sort, flashes a not-at-all nervy smile. A large part of the woman's brain goes into overdrive.

When things work out for a woman in Wales, man-wise, she switches Phases. (Most women consider this an upward move.) Her social life changes accordingly.

Firstly: there's the introduction of a few women, who the woman may not like in the least, but who she knows will make better friends than foes. She puts a fair bit of her energy into trying to make sure that this is the case.

EXAMPLES OF BETTER FRIENDS THAN FOES WOMEN

- Mothers-in-law (distant potential counts)
- Any woman with whom a woman's man works closely
- Any woman with whom a woman's man has a long-standing friendship
- A man's sister
- A man's daughter (smart daughters, over the age of three, are not above milking this situation for all it's worth)

After a while a woman gets fed up with having to pander. She lets off a bit of steam with a sympathetic chum. ('She is *sooo* spoilt.')

And then, she takes it all out on some woman, with whom the man has previously had a perfectly satisfactory, envelope-note relationship ... 'Honestly, darling, that loo hasn't seen bleach since the year dot. Get Rid Of Her ...'

Secondly, a woman, eventually, tires of showing a New Man off to her single chums. Apart from the fact that she doesn't want to push her luck, with regard to the 'not really fanciable' verdict, she thinks that it would be more fun to do things 'as a couple' with other couples.

Luckily, a woman with any kind of man at all often discovers that it's down to her to do most of the organising, socially speaking, so there's no problem with making paired-off plans.

When a woman's best friend has a New Man (who was *not* sourced via the friend's man's filofax), two men, who have never met, can find themselves making small-talk over a smoking barbecue quicker than you can say: 'How's next weekend for you?'

Generally, a bit of a Man United related forty-five minuter ensues.

OTHER PAIRED-OFF PLANS

* Dinner parties

Dinner parties are severely affected by Crazes. Six people can find themselves tucking into more balsamic vinegar than they've previously eaten in their lives, over a period of three Saturday nights, quicker than you can say ... 'Did you see Delia?'

When the Couple are all alone and not bothering with Tuscan Tomatoes they make do with a bit of pasta.

Quite late one Friday night a woman is unpacking some essentials from an Eight 'til Late plastic sack. This woman, if pressed, might not say her life was lovely exactly, but she'd certainly say things are not going too badly. She can hardly

71

remember what a Hideously Lonely weekend is like. Work doesn't seem so bad these days and she has lots of lady chums. ('Tom's away on Wednesday and Thursday, what do you fancy?')

Also, it isn't so long since she and Tom and some other couple had an *amazing* holiday Somewhere Sunny.

The woman smiles at the recollection of the *amazing* holiday just as she gives the bleach cupboard a shove with her foot. Tom is watching her.

He smiles too. He says: 'Come and sit down.'

The woman says: 'Just let me take off my coat.'

Tom says: 'Come and sit down.' He sounds serious.

The woman smiles a slight nervy smile and follows Tom to the sofa.

Once she's settled in Tom starts saying something which is a major step towards marriage. This takes a while but, eventually, the woman gets the gist. Kilos start dropping off her like ninepins.

Not very long after this happens to a woman she is absolutely desperate to have a good gas with pretty much every other woman she has ever met. Mothers and sisters usually come first on the list but she works her way through to the Aroma/Colour/Acu Therapist with a rapidity which takes your average Tom by surprise.

A great girls' restaurant lunch ensues. Some really serious shopping takes place after that. The shopping goes on for months, actually. During these months Nano-Zanosphere's recommendations and high hair hopes flow down the phone lines. Then one of the Pasta Party pals figures that it's down to her to organise a major Full Set female get together. A hen night.

On hen nights some women fancy acting like cocks. This involves watching people get their gear off and lots of saucy talk. With props.

Some women prefer a dressed-up-to-the-absolute-nines/hit the town with a ton of hairspray/adventure. (Lots of snagged tights and one-more-drink laughs.)

Some women decide that a restaurant might be fun.

('Ooh, no, let's not go there again.')

Sometimes one of the women just thinks 'what the hell' and invites everyone to her place.

At the hen party all the women from all the Phases are united.

Plenty of hugs are had.

One of the women settles herself well into the sofa as soon as she's taken off her coat. This woman has gained a *lot* of kilos since she last saw all her chums. Most of these kilos are *not* on her bottom.

Everyone can see them.

15

Breeding Marvellous

....

'You left your yoghurt in the bathroom'

....

Pregnancy takes sofa talk to whole new depths. Women who are in a step-towards-getting-pregnant are rather more fascinated by the *Details* than women who are not. In a mixed group the expression 'aaagh ...' tends to crop up more than frequently. Face pulling and leg crossing ensues. Still, pretty much everyone is interested in the gist.

A non-medical man who knows a great deal about the reproductive organs of other men is generally a man whose interest in other men extends beyond the platonic.

It's different with women. Women talk below the belt for years before they've got babies on the brain. Menstruation kicks things off.

MENSTRUAL BONDING: TEEN YEARS

- Using the same kind of sanitary protection
- Buying it together
- Going to the loo together after they've bought it
- Sympathising on sports day

Even when women are way past their teens, menstrual empathy rules.

If two women (who were introduced in a pub in Wales an hour and a half earlier) should find themselves coming out of cubicles and reaching for their combs at the same time, one of them could say to the other: '*Hideous* cramps' and the other one would pick up the thread.

Women who've known each other for longer than an hour and a half might say a good deal more to each other on a cramp day.

The expression 'You do not look fat' is a feature.

The sofa sharing of info on the Female Ailments and Physiology front, tends to relate to Phases. No one under forty mentions the menopause.

About town girls in the Men stage talk STDs timidly. ('But I mean, you might get it some other way ... right?')

Paired Off (thinking-about-it) pals might *tête à tête* re endometriosis or ectopics.

Women ensconced in kiddie land can chat prolapses and placentas without even pausing to squirm.

> When a woman needs to know about thrush or fissures or cystitis or caesareans, she doesn't have to go to the library.

When a woman's close friends start having babies she often feels like this: DESPERATE to have a baby too.

Lots of women suspect that making 'Let's get pregnant together' pacts is a bit daft. Lots of women do it anyway. Under circumstances like these the desperation can get a bit intensified.

Sometimes a woman isn't at all DESPERATE. Sometimes she is CONVINCED that having babies is the death knell for women.

Mostly, though, a woman charts a middle course. Mostly, a woman would just Quite Like to have a baby. Because:

- She likes babies
- She is in love with a man who likes babies
- She is in love with a man who doesn't like babies
- She has just had a birthday which started with a three
- She'd like to be Kept [Variation (a) She hates her job; Variation (b) She has no job]
- *Everyone* else is doing it

When a woman first sees her friend's baby she looks down at its teeny, tiny fingernails and says: 'She's *adooorable.*'
  Sometimes she has a wee teary in the eye.

All of the above is intensified times one million and four if the women concerned are sisters.
  Mums just cry and hug a lot. (All Girls Together Mums say 'I am *never* going to be called *Nana.*')

Babied and Baby-less women do stay friends ('Will you be her godmother?').

But there are some minor tensions.

Some minor tensions which develop between Babied and Baby-less women friends ...

Babies turn into Toddlers.

> Other people's babies are either boring, adorable or mildly Irritating (when crying).
> All Toddlers are wilful, demanding, exhausting and *mobile*.

A Babied friend visiting a Baby-less friend can leave said baby in a Moses basket. If it cries she can invoke awe and respect by baring her breast to it. Even the most inept person can hold a baby if they are settled into a sofa corner first. Babies might cry but they *do not* throw Lego.

TODDLERS

- grind biscuit into the carpet
- demand juice to go with the biscuit
- drop juice on the carpet
- knock things over and break them
- scream at the top of their lungs when this happens
- pull hair (yours)
- torment cats (yours)
- scream at the top of their lungs when the cat acts in self-defence.

Their mothers say:
'Naaaasty cat ... horrible pussy cat.'
Which is pretty bloody irritating.

THEN TODDLERS

- hurl themselves, with complete disregard for their safety, from the top of the steps (yours)
- scream at the top of their lungs when they land on their heads.

Their mothers screech:
'Those steps are *so* dangerous. I can't *believe* you've never had them *fixed*' and rush off home with their precious bundles and a car load full of Stuff. (This Stuff is always minus a few parts which are left in your sofa.)

The Baby-less woman who wants to avoid the wedge that this sort of tension might drive between her and her Babied friend takes an awfully cute present for the Toddler next time she sees her friend.

Since Baby-less women are jolly popular choices for God-mothers she is probably already signed up to buying awfully cute (and progressively more expensive) presents for the kid anyhow.

Little Note ...
Toddlers grow into people. This process seems to take longer than it actually does but, eventually, the cat-torturer grows into a small person. This small person is capable of kissing someone, in an awfully sweet way, and saying something like: 'I love you Aunty Kate.'

This type of behaviour can have a terrifically cementing effect on the relationships of grown-up women.

16

Growing Pains

....

'And I am never going to give them guns'
'Never'
'And you can forget *lugging all that stuff around'*
'Absolutely'
'And, my *children are going to eat healthy, nutritious food ... none of this fish fingers nonsense'*
'Definitely'

....

Women who have a baby on the same day in the same ward in the same hospital often form a Christmas card bond which lasts a lifetime.

Actually, babies are bonding generally. Because the mum of someone young usually finds that no matter how often Baby-less friends say: 'Ooh, I don't mind ... honestly', she is more relaxed sitting on a sofa which is already loaded down with Lego.

Also, if you're living in leggings, even the oldest pal can seem a bit Irritating when she shows up in an immaculate mono-chrome outfit.

So, mums of someone young tend to become day-to-day-really-good-chums with women who are in the same boat-in-the-bath-tub phase.

Friendships like these are often for life but, as the Toddler stage (and car seat Craze) draws to a close there is a bit of a thinning-out process.

Comparison of apple juice brands can only sustain a conversation for so long. Once there are no more cat-torturers constantly interrupting the conversation, to demand said apple juice, this fact becomes obvious.

The expression 'Thank God' frequently leaps to the lips of women whose children have begun to have birthdays beginning with more than a three.

Then again ...

Some modern women have babies, spend a few months in which nipples feature in a pretty major way, and then drag themselves back to their desks. From dawn 'til dark.

Others just settle in to being Kept. For ever.

Most women manage a middle course. Their lives are soon divided into equal parts Kids/Career/Crises/Exhaustion. They get used to it.

They say: 'It's worth it ... really.'

They say this to each other with a slight nervy edge in their voices.

Whatever route they choose, the majority of mothers eventually reach a point when they can have a chat with a chum, or a chap at the office, or a check-out operator at Whole-Healthy Foods, which *doesn't* have Children in it.

Some mums don't.

Some women develop an Interest in their offspring which goes way beyond caring.

A woman gets an inkling that her friend may never come up for air when all their conversations start to become three way.

A person who casually introduces the subject of, say, black holes to a woman who is suffering from Maternal Mental Meltdown finds that this woman turns away and says: 'What do we think of *that* then ... ?'

She says this, in a very silly voice, to someone who has no control over their own bodily functions.

Once upon a time a woman had a bit of a celebratory lunch with her work mates. She'd spent the morning saying *sayonara* to her phone friends. She was in her second trimester.

Over lunch the women had a bit of a giggly gas about nipples and nausea and then they turned their attention to the future. The words 'part' and 'time' popped up. Everyone said 'Perfect'. At this point in her life the woman had a detailed image of her future (herself, her home and her offspring) which doesn't quite tally with how things are today.

Today the mum of someone young is feeling pretty exhausted. The someone young is sleeping it off. This woman suspects that the lovely Leaving Lunch happened to another woman in another lifetime. If pressed she'd say it was worth it. Still, she'd rather like someone to reassure her of this.

She phones a friend. This friend is in the same boat. They have a bit of a gas. One of them mentions someone from the old gang. They decide that they haven't seen *anyone* for ages. One of them suggests that maybe she ought to organise a bit of a reunion.

'*What* a good idea,' says the chum. She sounds enthusiastic. She says she's had it with leggings and Lego and she just fancies a day out. It's on.

Lots of phone calls ensue. Mothers and 'my' childminders are high on the list.

Someone calls Meltdown Mama. *No one* has seen her for ages.

Meltdown Mama isn't sure she can make it. 'I don't like to leave her ...'

Meltdown Mama doesn't respond favourably to sharing offers of mothers and 'my' childminders. Eventually, after lots more phone calls, someone rings back and says: 'Bring her then, no one will mind ...'

The women meet at a girls' restaurant. No one is late. They are all in very high spirits. They tell each other that they look fantastic and everybody hugs like mad.

Nobody says a word about the fact that there is a three-year-old removing olives from a little dish in the middle of the table, throwing them on the floor and grinding them into the carpet with her heel.

One of the people who doesn't say a word is the child's mother. It isn't long before a fair bit of eye-rolling is going on.

Afterwards the phone rings hot: 'Could you *believe* it ...?'

Intelligent people *do* understand that tiny tots can't see reason.

What they *don't* understand is a fully grown adult woman who gets down on her knees in the super-market to test this theory:

'Now, darling, you *know* Mummy doesn't like it when you do that ...'

The thing is that three-year-olds who pick up the fact that at least one fully grown adult person will drop to her knees at the slightest provocation tend to turn into long-term Monster Olive Throwers.

Meltdown Mama isn't the only kind of mother who ever finds herself with a Monster Olive Thrower (or worse, three) on her hands.

All mothers with any Monster Olive Throwers at all soon find that their social circle is severely limited.

Sometimes a woman who is raising an Olive Thrower or three discovers that it isn't only her women friends who stop popping by. ('Well, it would be nice to see her, but those *children*.')

Sometimes the Meltdown Mama's Man gets fed up with schlepping home only to have olives thrown at him.

For a long time he tolerates this state of affairs. He simply buries himself in Man United related activities at every opportunity.

One day Meltdown Mama's man meets someone who sucks her olives, provocatively, off a cocktail stick and doesn't mention children at all ...

17

Down Time

'Do you pay into a pension plan?'
'No, I can't afford it'
'Me neither'
Pause
'What are you wearing to Kath's party?'
'Well, you know that black top I bought? ...
I thought I'd look for some trousers to go with it'

Nowadays most women get as far as Phases One and Two
i.e.

Working Girl	Clothes Phase
Men	Social Phase

During the second of these, lots of them have a bit of a mini nervous breakdown.

It is always brought on by some Man.

It is often exacerbated by some Unsympathetic Boss.

It is almost always relieved (at least a bit) by some Jolly Supportive, 'Let's go shopping/partying' chum(s). (Mothers are often no damn use at all.)

When women are having this breakdown they think that they are as unhappy as they could possibly be.

Some girls say this (to their chum(s)): 'I wish I could just *die*.'

Some girls mean it.

The thing is ... THEY AIN'T SEEN NOTHIN' YET

Even when girls get grown up, men go on featuring in their nervous breakdowns. Sometimes a man's behaviour is as far from gentlemanly as it could possibly be. Sometimes a man falls prey to a man stealer. Sometimes things aren't nearly so dramatic.

Once upon a time a woman had a bit of a celebratory evening with all her chums. She'd spent the afternoon doing some serious spending in White Frock Shops. She was engaged.

During the evening the girls had a bit of a giggly gas about husbands and honeymoons and then they turned their attention to the future. The words 'for' and 'ever' popped up. Everybody smiled. Perfect. At this point in her life the woman had a detailed image of her future (herself, her home, her husband) which doesn't quite tally with how things are today.

Today the husband's wife is feeling pretty exhausted. She hasn't had much sleep. The husband is sleeping soundly. This woman suspects that the Happy Hen Night happened to another woman in another lifetime. If pressed she'd probably say 'Oh ... we're fine.'

The wife looks at her husband and thinks: 'There is no *passion* at all any more. At best we're just good friends.'

A woman's Man Status often changes pretty dramatically, soon after she starts to think like this.

> *Women say:*
> 'Why can't I have the sort of relationship with a Man that I have with my girlfriends?'
>   They say this until they do.

If a woman puts a decade or two of her life into Achieving on the Man Status front, to the detriment of her own 1) interests 2) income, only to discover that her Man Status is standing at an all-time low, she tends to wake up on weekends feeling pretty grim.

If this woman has established friendships with other women based largely on Comparable Man Status, grim could give way to absolutely ghastly, before she's even hurled the balsamic vinegar across the kitchen.

Smart women know that entwining their lives with a man's can be a lot of fun for all concerned.
   It's the Revolving Around business that does people in.

A grown up girl's Man Status doesn't have to take a dive, her nerves can give way anyway ...

Once upon a time a woman spent a bit of a celebratory weekend at home. Some chums had come, sisters too. She was twenty-one.
   There was gassing and giggling and toasting the future. The words 'whole' and 'life' were mentioned. A lot. At this point the twenty-one-year-old had a detailed image of herself which tallies *exactly* with how things are today ...

When a woman has been having birthdays which begin with a three for a fair old while she tends *not* to want to find herself *still* in Phase Two.

A woman who has put a decade or more of her life into: not-ending-up-like-her-mother, often has second thoughts when her thirties are whizzing by.

Of course, if pressed by her mother, she'd say 'I'm absolutely fine.'

One day a woman decides that she can't face another same-sort-of-day at work. She can't face any more same-old-stuff on the telly either, so, she lies in late, with the covers over her head. She thinks back to the days when a new pair of over-the-knee boots seemed like the solution to all her woes. Her mind trawls through all the Crazes that came after the over-the-knee boots. She decides that, despite the different hairdos, she hasn't got *anywhere*.

Eventually she gets up, and goes downstairs to check the machine. (Expecting the office.) She ignores the first same-old-problems-with-assistants message. The second message gets her thinking. It's Gentleman Jim.

This woman has been dating Gentleman Jim for a fair old while. (Gentleman Jim has outlasted a fair few newer, rat-bag, rivals.) If pressed, the woman would say: 'There's no *passion* ... but we're pretty good friends.'

Suddenly, this little thought pops out of the woman's subconscious: 'Perhaps, if I *married* him ...'

The woman conjures up an image of life as the wife of Gentleman Jim. She can't quite see it. Still, she doesn't give up on the idea entirely.

Later that afternoon the phone rings. The woman picks it up as soon as she hears a friend's voice on the answering machine amplifier. The friend explains that she tried the office.

The friend says:

'You seem a bit low.'

The woman says:

'Yes, I am a bit.'

In woman-speak this is code for:

a) I am absolutely miserable
b) I am desperately lonely
c) I am terrified of the future
d) I don't love my husband (plus a and c)
e) I love my husband but he doesn't love me (plus a, b, and c)
f) I don't have a man (plus a, b, and c)
g) I have a man but he doesn't want to be my husband (plus a and c)

Another woman can usually pick up the thread.

The conversation continues like this:

'Ooh, do you fancy getting out? We could go to the cinema ... and have supper afterwards.'

Then the blue woman, nine times out of ten, says: 'I shouldn't really. I'm a bit broke' (variant: 'She cut up my card right in front of me').

Now then, this doesn't mean that rich women don't get the blues, they do. It's just that the blue and broke scenario is awfully common (if you were to add single and/or baby to this equation you'd be on to a fairly sure thing).

Years and years of treading water at work, and spending the gas bill money on sling-backs, and shelling out fortunes for Nano-Zanospheres, and taking off Somewhere Sunny on a whim has its price.

More women than will ever admit it offload responsibility for this state of affairs onto Men. They wail to a pal: 'I thought we were getting *married*.'

In an absolutely worst case blaming-blokes scenario a woman is not above trotting out this old chestnut: 'I thought when he knew about the baby ...'

18

Intensive Care

....

When a woman shares a problem with a man, the man thinks he is supposed to fix it. He asks her a load of questions to assist him with this process.

The woman ends up having a bit of a row with him about why the problem occurred in the first place.

When a woman shares a problem with another woman, the other woman gets out a tub of Haagen-Daz and two spoons.

....

Of course it's not just Men and Money that get women down.

Children can be special-case causes of women's nervous breakdowns: Not being able to have them/something unthinkable happening to them. Under these circumstances a woman usually has a terribly sad man to be Best Friends with.

They both need lots of people to be Best Friends with them. Sisters often turn out to be more helpful than anyone could have possibly imagined.

Sometimes a woman wakes up with a worst case scenario. This is the day her friends say: 'It makes you realise, health is everything.'

Hopefully they do.

When the friend on the phone hears that the friend at home is having a bout of the lower-mid-level blues (men, money, extremely distant potential with regard to promotion or popping off Somewhere Sunny) she says she'll come round after work. She'll bring some supper.

At 7 pm hugs are had, flowers are exchanged, and the visiting friend takes charge. She gets the blue chum settled into the sofa and pours her a glass of wine. The blue chum tucks her legginged legs up underneath her and watches the Eight 'til Late stash get unpacked. The friend has splashed out. There's pudding.

The blue chum starts to feel a bit better. The friend relates an incident-at-the-office tale. A Swotty-bossy type and an utterly useless assistant are key players. The friend does actions. There's eye-rolling.

By the time she gets to the bit where the utterly useless assistant is pouting behind her partition and the Swotty-bossy type is huffily tippexing initials onto her stapler, the mood has lightened up all round.

The evening follows a fairly standard sort of sofa-night procedure. The women have a bit of a laugh and a woe swap. Suddenly, the friend grabs her handbag and starts rooting around in it. She says: 'I've brought the I Ching.'

The other woman is thrilled.

When an intelligent modern woman consults the I Ching, or the Astral Almanac or the Telephone Tarot, what she is looking for is a bit of encouraging news re the men, money, promotion or popping off to Somewhere Sunny potential, in her very near future.

Women tend not to admit to men, or women who aren't their friends, just how often they do this.

The friend spends a few minutes getting to grips with all the bits and pieces. Eventually they're off. Both women stare in awed silence.

The previously glum chum says: 'What does it *mean*?'

The friend spends a few minutes getting to grips with what it means. Then she says: 'It means ... that you are at a fork in, um, the road, of your life ... and you have to, you know, choose where to go from here.'

And the chum says: 'That is *soo* true ...'

And the friend says: 'Ooh, no ... hang on, that wasn't it ...'

After this, a jolly good time is had until the mini-cab arrives.

When a woman's blues get below lower-mid-level mark she needs a mate who's a Real Brick.

Some behavioural clues to much lower than mid-level mark blues

Losing it with assistants at tights counters
Losing it with parking-space stealers
Losing it when the butter dish breaks
Crying
Crying
Crying
Crying
Crying
Getting too blue to cry any more

All this is a bit wearing on the Real Brick (especially when the miserable mate loses it with *her*) but she soldiers on.

The Real Brick keeps cooking and visiting and listening until the occasional crying break is viewed on the horizon (sometimes this can take an age) and then she is terribly pleased and the women have a bit of a hug and maybe even the odd laugh and they have a special bond between them for an awfully long time afterwards. (For *ever*, if they know what's good for them.)

Apart from I Ching chums and Real Bricks there are two other types of friends who pop up whenever a True Blue drama is being played out: Me Too's and Bad News Buddies.

Me Too's and Bad News Buddies are indistinguishable, at first, from Real Bricks so the rest of the Bunch say: 'Hasn't Cathy been a real brick since Kate's husband left?' They feel a bit relieved that *someone* has.

It is normal and pretty sensible to find endless crying rather a drag, but, beyond this, there are some women who are afraid that the blues might be catching. These women are dead keen on keeping the infectious woman in quarantine. They limit their condolences to the sterile end of a telephone line.

Me Too's

Love a spot of endless crying. Me Too's just bunker right down and cry too. Me Too's are disappointed with life (particularly Men). They're always pleased to have someone in the club with them. They don't miss a beat when someone says: 'I thought when I told him about the baby ...' A Me Too in the vicinity is likely to severely curtail the likelihood of any Crying Breaks appearing on the horizon.

If a Truly Blue wakes up one morning and decides that better times might be up ahead, the Me Too loses interest pretty damn quick.

She goes off in search of a New Best Friend.

Bad News Buddies

Can sniff out misery at a hundred paces. They head right for it. The Bad News Buddy is a babe who, if pressed, hard, *might* admit that the word 'lonely' would crop up rather more frequently than the word 'lovely' in a description of her life. The Bad News Buddy doesn't have to face up to this fact too often, though, because she manages to keep herself busy-busy-busy most of the time with some poor poppet who's *really* in the pits.

A woman, who's been blue-blue-blue, finds that a previously pretty distant pal starts stopping by like clockwork. The previously pretty distant pal doesn't seem to mind about the crying. In fact, she tells the woman to go right ahead. It's not long before she's telling her what to wear and when to go to bed. The weak-with-woe woman is grateful for the patience and the pasta and the pillow puffing.

She's much too miserable for the question: 'Whatever Happened To Baby Jane?' to pop into her head.

Bad News Buddies don't stay friends with fully recovered True Blues. Bad News Buddies are off Double Acting with an incurable.

19

Get Fresh

I've given up all unsaturated fats, and from now on I'm doing thirty-five sit-ups every weekday morning, and I'm going to go to the gym, and swim, on the weekends'

Women are great believers in the New Leaf/New Look/New Life formula

Some women are having lunch. They're loving it. They're tucking in to hunky chunks of something frito and sloshing it down with Chablis. One of them says: 'Well, it'll be brown rice and water tomorrow, girls.'

Laughs and mock moans ensue.

Chums who've come this far deserve some fun. These women have decided to treat themselves to the ultimate extra-bits-of-bottom-beating break. With Nano-Zanospheres. They're off to see some wizards in white coats who'll dust them down, brush them up and start them all over again.

These days, a woman doesn't have to surrender her freedom in order to have her thighs electrified or her face cemented over. Modern women can pay good money for an afternoon's worth of this stuff any old day of the week. Lots of them do.

Still, more and more women fancy going the whole health farm hog. They resolve to emerge from this experience all new and thin as pins. But more than their Demi Moore look-alike progress is at stake. Women often imagine that four days of algae, aerobics and all-fibre fodder will refocus their minds. They think that by the time they come home life will look lovelier.

'What time's your Tummy Pummel?'

'Eight o'clock. No ... hang on, that can't be right ... in the *morning*?'

On the first day, the women find that their resolve is a wee bit wavery. Still, they egg each other on. Anyway, when they get to breakfast (seven o'clock), there isn't a waffle in sight, so the caving opportunities are limited.

The women decide that they ought to take full advantage of their four full days of beauty-body treats, so they sign up for *everything*. They race from mud scrubs to massages. They rush from the jacuzzi to the gym. Their bathrobes are constantly flapping behind them. Sometimes they run into one another in the steam room. There's just time for a quick comparison of Cucumber Wrinkle Cures.

'It *feels* amazing.'

At seven o'clock (in the evening) they wolf down their rice and water with gusto. Not long after this they decide to skip the 'Yoga and You' talk. They decide to have a fairly early night. They drag themselves off to their little beds and tumble in without even pretending to look at their books. This pattern repeats itself for several days. Without variation.

At the end of the Total Beauty Body Treat, the women are a bit sorry to have to put on clothes with waistbands again. (This happens even if a woman has only spent an hour and a half, on a Tuesday, having herself pampered whilst slipped into something more comfortable.) They are convinced, though, that these waist-bands are feeling rather loose. They tell each other so.

The women hand over a hunky chunk of their salaries. (This happens even if a woman has only spent an hour and a half on a Tuesday having her shins sugared.) They are convinced, though, that it was worth it. They tell each other so.

The women have a hug in the car park. They say 'call me soon.' Two of them are sharing a car. They get in. The one whose car it isn't absent-mindedly scoffs a sticky toffee from the open bag on the dash. The driver follows suit. She starts the car.

There is a distinct absence of any gassing. This is partly due to the particular stickiness of the toffee. Also, both women are having a bit of a think. They are thinking about the lives that they are going back to.

When a woman finds herself heading home after a few days away, she often does a spot of reassessing. (An entirely new skin, new bottom or new hairdo intensifies this situation.) Women who find their lives wanting at a point like this have two options.

One of the women gazes steadily out of the car window, but the Welcome Break billboards barely dent her consciousness. This woman has decided that her life is not as lovely as it could be. She has decided that having Gentleman Jim's pyjamas under the pillow next to hers for forty years will *not* alleviate this situation.

This woman sits up in her seat, sucks hard on her toffee and resolves to have a damn good go at figuring out what *will*.

The driving pal sighs. She has decided that life is not as lovely as it could be, too. She figures that a coffee and a Mars bar might help. She keeps a keen eye out for Welcome Break billboards.

The women stop at the Welcome Break. One of them goes to the loo while the other one queues for coffees. They're still fairly subdued. They decide that all that last-minute fun on the sunbeds this morning has done them in. They decide to head for home fairly smartish. They get back in the car. From that moment on they are moving in opposite directions.

When an intelligent woman gets her mind into the right-hand lane for some fairly determined spurts, the results can be stratospheric.

New body, new baby, new man aren't in it.

This woman wants a New Plane. She wants to fly it herself.

Of course, sometimes, a woman just happens to be looking her Demi Moorish best, and she is standing in the supermarket queue when Robert Redford walks by and says: 'Hey, wanna play a wildly dangerous-to-know dame in my new movie?' and the woman says yes, and it turns out that she is an *amazing* actress, and she wins an Oscar, and she gets to wear that fab black evening frock she bought in the summer sales (as yet unworn) and Liam Neeson gives her a lift in his limo and ...

But, more often, when a woman starts living her dreams, she's working at it.

The funny thing is that once a woman starts heading, hard, towards a New Plane ... new men, new money and some fabulously glamorous new career opportunities often pop right up in front of her. (A new body and a new baby aren't out of the question.) There's something else that a woman bumps into on the road to a lovelier life, some new friends.

A happy chick can chum around with someone glum. But, if the glum chum *keeps* relying on Mars bars and coffee for crying relief the happy chick eventually becomes aware of the gulf between them.

Of course, sometimes a woman has just won an Oscar and is dating Liam Neeson so she needs to jet off Somewhere Sunny (fab black jacket/Raybans) immediately, in order to escape the press, which is why she is seeing a lot less of her old muckers ...

But, more often, when women slip out of one another's lives it's because they've taken different forks in the road.

If one of them has taken this fork arm in arm with the other one's man the split is fairly clear cut.

If both women have taken the same road but one of them has managed to race ahead, they just try to forget that the other one was ever there Whatever the reason for the parting of the ways it's fairly tough on all concerned. This is why:

When a woman breaks up with a man, who she's known for six months, she can have a right moan about him to all her friends.

Everyone is sympathetic. No one even minds if she has a wee weep. Eventually, she manages to wash that man right out of her brand new hairdo.

When a woman breaks up with a woman, who she has known for six years, and then some, she needs to keep pretty shtum (man-stealing would be an exception here) because whatever she says will sound like *bitching*. The woman worries that this bitching will spread. She worries that other women will gossip and judge and take sides.

A woman is not always way off the mark with this particular concern.

When a woman has a bust up with another woman, a man just doesn't want to know.

20

Ain't She Sweet?

....

'Have another chocolate, doll'

....

Once upon an awful time some girls turned their backs on another girl in the school corridor. They were fourteen. There was giggling and eye-rolling. Some wicked words popped up. Everybody sneered.

Yesterday, the girl with hurt in her eyes, was their friend.

The thing is, women *never* forget how to do this stuff.

On the whole women don't wallop. They have witchier methods at their disposal. Women know that a well-aimed whisper at a back inflicts just as much pain as a punch in the nose. Luckily, mostly, grown-up women get wise. If pressed re the corridor incident they wince. They're ashamed. They're never quite so evil again. If they *should* happen to find a teeny bit of ill will wiggling, and tickling, and giggling inside them, they take it out on someone they've never met.

'Did you see her on the telly this morning?'

'Oooh, I *know,* could you *believe* that frock?' for about forty-five minutes.

Then they get on with being pretty nice to each other and having some *really* good times.

Some things women do when they're having a really good time

- Dance
- Sing along together to songs that remind them of something
- Tell each other what this something is
- Laugh
- Swap funny stories (with actions)
- Say: 'Remember that guy ... yes you do ... with the glasses' and tell some more funny stories and laugh some more
- Eat. Heaps
- Not care about eating heaps.

Once upon a time, two women moved into adjacent houses. They were newlyweds. The word coffee popped up more than frequently. Twenty years later, they knew exactly where the other one kept the sugar.

Today, life keeps women out of each other's kitchens rather more than it used to. But still, some friends are for ever.

Every now and then a lucky woman comes across a Good Egg. Good Eggs do this:

- Encourage other women. Whatever.
- Allow other women their privacy. (No gossiping.)
- Allow other women to really open up. (No judging.)

Good Eggs have a lot of Good Times. *They deserve to.*

Swing Out Sister.

In a Great Friendship

Bosoms are no big deal